A Pocket Treasury *of*
IRISH
VERSE

DEDICATION
for Rachel

EDITOR
Fleur Robertson

PHOTOGRAPHY
© Michael Diggin Photography
Additional photography pp 36, 56: Digital Vision; p 44: CLB International

DESIGN
Louise Clements

PRODUCTION
Ruth Arthur, Karen Staff, Neil Randles

DIRECTOR OF PRODUCTION
Gerald Hughes

CLB 5046
© 1998 CLB International

Published in Ireland by
Gill & Macmillan Ltd, Goldenbridge, Dublin 8
with associated companies throughout the world

ISBN 0 7171 2681 1

Printed in Singapore

ENDPAPERS: Coumhoola Valley, Co. Cork
PREVIOUS PAGE: Portlaoise windowbox
THESE PAGES: cutting turf, Ring of Kerry

A Pocket Treasury *of*

IRISH
VERSE

GILL & MACMILLAN

CONTENTS

Sligo and Mayo

LOUIS MACNEICE

In Sligo the country was soft; there were turkeys
  Gobbling under sycamore trees
And the shadows of clouds on the mountains moving
  Like browsing cattle at ease.

And little distant fields were sprigged with haycocks
  And splashed against a white
Roadside cottage a welter of nasturtium
  Deluging the sight,

And pullets pecking the flies from around the eyes of heifers
  Sitting in farmyard mud
Among hydrangeas and the falling ear-rings
  Of fuchsias red as blood.

continued ...

FACING: *Classiebawn Castle, Mullaghmore, Co. Sligo*

But in Mayo the tumbledown walls went leap-frog
  Over the moors,
The sugar and salt in the pubs were damp in the casters
  And the water was brown as beer upon the shores

Of desolate loughs, and stumps of hoary bog-oak
  Stuck up here and there
As the twilight filtered on the heather
  Water-music filled the air,

And when the night came down upon the bogland
  With all-enveloping wings
The coal-black turfstacks rose against the darkness
  Like the tombs of nameless kings.

from *The Closing Album*

FACING: *Mayo waterfall*

The Lark in the Clear Air

SAMUEL FERGUSON

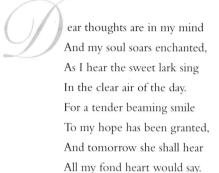

Dear thoughts are in my mind
And my soul soars enchanted,
As I hear the sweet lark sing
In the clear air of the day.
For a tender beaming smile
To my hope has been granted,
And tomorrow she shall hear
All my fond heart would say.

I shall tell her all my love,
All my soul's adoration;
And I think she will hear me
And will not say me nay.
It is this that fills my soul
With its joyous elation,
As I hear the sweet lark sing
In the clear air of the day.

FACING: *Aughascla Coumlocks, Co. Kerry*

Plough Horses

PATRICK KAVANAGH

Their glossy flanks and manes outshone
The flying splinters of the sun.

The tranquil rhythm of that team
Was as slow flowing meadow stream.

And I saw Phidias's chisel there –
An ocean stallion, mountain mare –

Seeing with eyes the Spirit unsealed
Plough horses in a quiet field.

Sonnet

CHARLES WOLFE

My spirit's on the mountains, where the birds
In wild and sportive freedom wing the air,
Amidst the heath-flowers and the browsing herds,
Where Nature's altar is, my spirit's there.
It is my joy to tread the pathless hills,
Though but in fancy – for my mind is free,
And walks by sedgy ways and trickling rills,
While I'm forbid the use of liberty.

This is delusion, but it is so sweet
That I could live deluded. Let me be
Persuaded that my springing soul may meet
The eagle on the hills – and I am free.
Who'd not be flatter'd by a fate like this?
To fancy is to feel our happiness.

FACING: *Glanmore Valley, Co. Kerry*

Plough Horses

PATRICK KAVANAGH

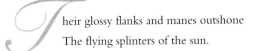heir glossy flanks and manes outshone
The flying splinters of the sun.

The tranquil rhythm of that team
Was as slow flowing meadow stream.

And I saw Phidias's chisel there –
An ocean stallion, mountain mare –

Seeing with eyes the Spirit unsealed
Plough horses in a quiet field.

ABOVE: *Knocknagoshel ploughing match, Co. Kerry*

The Short Cut to Rosses

NORA HOPPER CHESSON

By the short cut to Rosses a fairy girl I met;
I was taken by her beauty as a fish is in a net.
The fern uncurled to look at her, so very fair was she,
With her hair as bright as seaweed new-drawn from out the sea.

By the short cut to Rosses ('twas on the first of May)
I heard the fairies piping, and they piped my heart away;
They piped till I was mad with joy, but when I was alone
I found my heart was piped away and in my breast a stone.

By the short cut to Rosses 'tis I'll go never more
Lest I be robbed of soul by her that stole my heart before,
Lest she take my soul and crush it like a dead leaf in her hand,
For the short cut to Rosses is the way to Fairyland.

FACING: *the Rosses, Co. Donegal*

Prelude

J.M. SYNGE

*S*till south I went, and west, and south again,
Through Wicklow from the morning to the night,
And far from cities and the sights of men,
Lived with the sunshine and the moon's delight.

I knew the stars, the flowers and the birds,
The grey and wintry sides of many glens,
And did but half remember human words,
In converse with the mountains, moors and fens.

FACING: *Glendalough, Co. Wicklow*

Erin

THOMAS MOORE

Erin! the tear and the smile in thine eyes
Blend like the rainbow that hangs in thy skies!
Shining through sorrow's stream,
Saddening through pleasure's beam,
Thy sons, with doubtful gleam,
Weep while they rise!

Erin! thy silent tear never shall cease,
Erin! thy languid smile ne'er shall increase,
Till, like the rainbow's light,
Thy various tints unite,
And form, in Heaven's sight,
One arch of peace!

FACING: *a double rainbow over the River Blackwater, Fermoy, Co. Cork*

The Farmer's Son

T.D. SULLIVAN

Where'er are scattered the Irish nation,
In foreign lands or on Irish ground,
In every calling and rank and station
Good men and true will always be found:
  But 'midst their masses
  And ranks and classes,
When noble work must be dared and done,
  No heart's more ready,
  No hand's more steady
Than the heart and hand of a farmer's son.

His homely garb has not fashion's gaces,
But it wraps a frame that is lithe and strong;
His brawny hand may show labour's traces,
But 'tis honest toil that does no man wrong.
  For generous greeting,
  For social meeting,
For genial mirth or for harmless fun,
  'Midst high or low men,
  'Midst friend or foemen,
Oh where's the match for a farmer's son?

ABOVE: *a Kerry lad*

Kinsale

DEREK MAHON

The kind of rain we knew is a thing of the past —
deep-delving, dark, deliberate you would say,
browsing on spire and bogland; but today
our sky-blue slates are steaming in the sun,
our yachts tinkling and dancing in the bay
like race-horses. We contemplate at last
shining windows, a future forbidden to no-one.

FACING: *the harbour at Kinsale, Co. Cork*

Last Lines - 1916

PATRICK PEARSE

The beauty of the world hath made me sad,
This beauty that will pass;
Sometimes my heart hath shaken with great joy
To see a leaping squirrel in a tree,
Or a red lady-bird upon a stalk,
Or little rabbits in a field at evening,
Lit by a slanting sun,
Or some green hill where shadows drifted by
Some quiet hill where mountainy man hath sown
And soon would reap; near to the gate of Heaven;
Or children with bare feet upon the sands
Of some ebbed sea, or playing on the streets
Of little towns in Connacht,
Things young and happy.
And then my heart hath told me:
These will pass,
Will pass and change, will die and be no more,
Things bright and green, things young and happy;
And I have gone upon my way
Sorrowful.

ABOVE: *ladybird and leaf*

The Mystery

AMERGIN trans. by DOUGLAS HYDE

I am the wind which breathes upon the sea,

I am the wave of the ocean,

I am the murmur of the billows,

I am the ox of the seven combats,

I am the vulture on the rocks,

I am a beam of the sun,

I am the fairest of plants,

I am a wild boar in valour,

I am a salmon in the water,

I am a lake in the plain,

I am a word of science,

I am the point of the lance of battle,

I am the God who created in the head the fire.

Who is it who throws light into the meeting on the mountain?

Who announces the ages of the moon?

Who teaches the place where crouches the sun?

(If not I)

FACING: *Killorglin, Ring of Kerry*

The Little Waves *of* Breffny

EVA GORE-BOOTH

The grand road from the mountains goes shining to the sea,
And there is traffic in it and many a horse and cart,
But the little roads of Cloonagh are dearer far to me,
And the little roads of Cloonagh go rambling through my heart.

A great storm from the ocean goes shouting o'er the hill,
And there is glory in it and terror on the wind,
But the haunted air of twilight is very strange and still,
And the little winds of twilight are dearer to my mind.

The great waves of the Atlantic sweep storming on the way,
Shining green and silver with the hidden herring shoal,
But the little waves of Breffny have drenched my heart in spray.
And the little waves of Breffny go stumbling through my soul.

FACING: *west coast waves*

ABOVE: *a white hybrid tea rose*

A White Rose

JOHN BOYLE O'REILLY

The red rose whispers of passion,
And the white rose breathes of love;
Oh, the red rose is a falcon,
And the white rose is a dove.

But I send you a cream-white rose-bud
With a flush on its petal tips;
For the love that is purest and sweetest
Has a kiss of desire on the lips.

The Rose *of* Tralee

WILLIAM PEMBROKE MULCHINOCK

The pale moon was rising above the green mountain,
The sun was declining beneath the blue sea,
When I stray'd with my love to the pure crystal fountain
That stands in the beautiful vale of Tralee.

She was lovely and fair as the rose of the summer,
Yet 'twas not her beauty alone that won me,
Oh no, 'twas the truth in her eyes ever beaming
That made me love Mary, the Rose of Tralee.

The cool shades of evening their mantle were spreading,
And Mary, all smiling, was list'ning to me,
The moon through the valley her pale rays was shedding
When I won the heart of the Rose of Tralee.

Tho' lovely and fair as the rose of the summer,
Yet 'twas not her beauty alone that won me,
Oh no, 'twas the truth in her eyes ever beaming
That made me love Mary, the Rose of Tralee.

ABOVE: *Tralee Bay, Co. Kerry*

He Wishes for the Cloths *of* Heaven

W.B. YEATS

Had I the heavens' embroidered cloths,
Enwrought with golden and silver light,
The blue and the dim and the dark cloths
Of night and light and the half-light,
I would spread the cloths under your feet:
But I, being poor, have only my dreams;
I have spread my dreams under your feet;
Tread softly because you tread on my dreams.

FACING: *oncoming rain, Co. Donegal*

My Own Land

ROBERT EMMET

This world hath many a glorious land,
Where beauty ever dwells,
Old snow-crowned hills, and rivers grand,
And happy summer dells.

Of these the Poet in his lays,
Loves evermore to tell,
Where heroes died in former days,
Where Freedom's martyrs fell.

But my own land is dearer far,
Than all, where'er they be,
My own land – my own land –
Is all the world to me.

FACING: *Caherconree Mountain, Dingle Peninsula*

ABOVE: *a warm welcome waiting, Dowlings pub*

Let Us Be Merry Before We Go

JOHN PHILPOT CURRAN

If sadly thinking, with spirits sinking,
Could, more than drinking, my cares compose
A cure for sorrow from sighs I'd borrow,
And hope tomorrow would end my woes.
But as in wailing there's nought availing,
And Death unfailing will strike the blow,
Then for that reason, and for a season,
Let us be merry before we go.

To joy a stranger, a wayworn ranger,
In every danger my course I've run;
Now hope all ending, and death befriending,
His last aid lending, my cares are done.
No more a rover, or hapless lover,
My griefs are over – my glass runs low;
Then for that reason, and for a season,
Let us be merry before we go.

The Lake Isle *of* Innisfree

W.B. YEATS

I will arise and go now, and go to Innisfree,
And a small cabin build there, of clay and wattles made;
Nine bean-rows will I have there, a hive for the honey bee,
And live alone in the bee-loud glade.

And I shall have some peace there, for peace comes
                                             dropping slow,
Dropping from the veils of the morning to where the
                                             cricket sings;
There midnight's all a glimmer, and noon a purple glow,
And evening full of the linnet's wings.

I will arise and go now, for always night and day
I hear lake water lapping with low sounds by the shore;
While I stand on the roadway, or on the pavements grey,
I hear it in the deep heart's core.

FACING: *lake water reflections*

Ireland

FRANCIS STUART

ver you falls the sea light, festive yet pale
As though from the trees hung candles alight in a gale
To fill with shadows your days, as the distant beat
Of waves fill the lonely width of many a western street.
Bare and grey and hung with berries of mountain ash,
Drifting through ages with tilted fields awash,
Steeped with your few lost lights in the long Atlantic dark,
Sea-birds' shelter, our shelter and ark.

FACING: *snow on the Dingle Peninsula*

Thatcher

SEAMUS HEANEY

Bespoke for weeks, he turned up some morning
Unexpectedly, his bicycle slung
With a light ladder and a bag of knives.
He eyed the old rigging, poked at the eaves,

Opened and handled sheaves of lashed wheat-straw.
Next, the bundled rods: hazel and willow
Were flicked for weight, twisted in case they'd snap.
It seemed he spent the morning warming up:

Then fixed the ladder, laid out well honed blades
And snipped at straw and sharpened ends of rods
That, bent in two, made a white-pronged staple
For pinning down his world, handful by handful.

Couchant for days on sods above the rafters
He shaved and flushed the butts, stitched all together
Into a sloped honeycomb, a stubble patch,
And left them gaping at his Midas touch.

FACING: *traditional Irish thatch*

Windharp

JOHN MONTAGUE

The sounds of Ireland,
that restless whispering
you never get away
from, seeping out of
low bushes and grass,
heatherbells and fern,
wrinkling bog pools,
scraping tree branches,
light hunting cloud,
sound hounding sight,
a hand ceaselessly
combing and stroking
the landscape, till
the valley gleams
like the pile upon
a mountain pony's coat.

FACING: *scene on the way to Glenbeigh, Co. Kerry*

The Singers

for Mary Robinson

EAVAN BOLAND

The women who were singers in the West
lived on an unforgiving coast.
I want to ask was there ever one
moment when all of it relented,
when rain and ocean and their own
sense of home were revealed to them
as one and the same?

                After which
every day was still shaped by weather,
but every night their mouths filled with
Atlantic storms and clouded-over stars
and exhausted birds.

                And only when the danger
was plain in the music could you know
their true measure of rejoicing in

finding a voice where they found a vision.

FACING: *a wild sea, West of Ireland*

Winter Morning

KATHARINE TYNAN

The stars faded out of a paling sky,
Dropped through the waters, but the Morning Star
Grew brighter and brighter, and as the day was nigh
A pure wind troubled the rushes near and far.

No bird was yet awake: only the duck
Homed to the little lake, fed full with streams:
Strange and unreal the full morning broke
On a still world as God saw it in dreams.

The still-life, austere world was grey and cool,
Lit by one burning torch of purest flame.
Home – from what hidden haunt, what secret pool? –
Borne on the morning wind, the wild duck came.

FACING: *winter lake, Co. Galway*

The Outlaw *of* Loch Lene

JEREMIAH JOSEPH CALLANAN

Oh, many a day have I made good ale in the glen,
That came not of stream or malt, like the brewing of men.
My bed was the ground, my roof the greenwood above,
And the wealth that I sought, one fair kind glance from my love.

Alas! on that night when the horses I drove from the field,
That I was not near from terror my angel to shield.
She stretched forth her arms – her mantle she flung to the wind –
And swam o'er Loch Lene her outlawed lover to find.

Oh, would that a freezing, sleet-winged tempest did sweep,
And I and my love were alone far off on the deep!
I'd ask not a ship, or a bark, or a pinnace to save;
With her hand round my waist I'd fear not the wind or the wave.

'Tis down by the lake where the wild tree fringes its sides
That maid of my heart, the fair one of heaven, resides;
I think as at eve she wanders its mazes along
The birds go to sleep by the sweet, wild twist of her song.

ABOVE: *Lough Leane, Killarney*

I Saw from the Beach

THOMAS MOORE

I saw from the beach, when the morning was shining,
A bark o'er the waters move gloriously on;
I came when the sun from that beach was declining,
The bark was still there, but the waters were gone.

And such is the fate of our life's early promise,
So passing the spring-tide of joy we have known;
Each wave that we danc'd on at morning ebbs from us,
And leaves us, at eve, on the bleak shore alone.

Ne'er tell me of glories, serenely adorning
The close of our day, the calm eve of our night; –
Give me back, give me back the wild freshness of Morning,
Her clouds and her tears are worth Evening's best light!

FACING: *wreck and deserted beach, West of Ireland*

Wind Song

JOHN TODHUNTER

*B*ring from the craggy haunts of birch and pine
    Thou wild wind, bring,
Keen forest odours from that realm of thine,
    Upon thy wing!

O wind, O mighty, melancholy wind,
    Blow through me, blow!
Thou blowest forgotten things into my mind
    From long ago.

FACING: *mountain mist*

Along the Path to the Vale

ROSA MULHOLLAND

The silent bird is hid in the boughs,
　　The scythe is hid in the corn,
The lazy oxen wink and drowse
　　The grateful sheep are shorn;
Redder and redder burns the rose,
　　The lily was ne'er so pale,
Stiller and stiller the river flows
　　Along the path to the vale.

A little door is hid in the boughs,
　　A face is hiding within;
When birds are silent and oxen drowse
　　Why should a maiden spin?
Slower and slower turns the wheel,
　　The face turns red and pale,
Brighter and brighter the looks that steal
　　Along the path to the vale.

FACING: *abandoned mountain cabin*

And That Being So

PAUL DURCAN

My soul is the High Meadow we played in,
My cousin and I, when we were young,
The High Meadow where we danced
Round a fairy ring.

My soul is the figure of my first love
Skipping quickly across the sands,
Her hair dyed yellow – was that wise? –
Round her laughing eyes.

But the High Meadow's been built upon
And that being so and my first love gone
My soul must step in the streets
Round the fire of song.

FACING: *Kerry peak*

ABOVE: *mute swan*

The Song *of* Fionnuala

THOMAS MOORE

Silent, O Moyle, be the roar of thy water;
Break not, ye breezes, your chain of repose,
While murmuring mournfully, Lir's lonely daughter
Tells to the night-star her tale of woes.
When shall the swan, her death-note singing,
Sleep, with wings in darkness furl'd?
When will heaven, its sweet bells ringing,
Call my spirit from this stormy world?

Sadly, O Moyle, to thy winter-wave weeping,
Fate bids me languish long ages away;
Yet still in her darkness doth Erin lie sleeping,
Still doth the pure light its dawning delay.
When will that day-star, mildly springing,
Warm our isle with peace and love?
When will heaven, its sweet bells ringing,
Call my spirit to the fields above?

An Old Tune

WILLIAM ALLINGHAM

*M*ongst the green Irish hills I love dearly,
At the close of the bright summer day,
I heard an old tune lilted clearly,
That soothed half my sorrows away.
And far o'er the wide-rolling ocean
Methinks I am hearing it now,
As a farewell of tender emotion –
'The Pretty Girl Milking her Cow'.

Next day was the last look of Erin;
'Twas almost like death to depart;
And since, in my foreign wayfaring,
That tune's like a thread round my heart.
Still back to the dear old Green Island
It draws me, I cannot tell how –
The whisper in music of my land –
'The Pretty Girl Milking her Cow'.

FACING: *the Caragh River, Iveragh Peninsula*

Frost

JOHN HEWITT

With frost again the thought is clear and wise
that rain made dismal with a mist's despair
the raw bleak earth beneath cloud-narrowed skies
finds new horizons in the naked air.
Light leaps along the lashes of the eyes;
a tree is truer for its being bare.

So must the world seem keen and very bright
to one whose gaze is on the end of things,
who knows, past summer lush, brimmed autumn's height,
no promise in the inevitable springs,
all stripped of shadow down to bone of light,
the false songs gone and gone the restless wings.

FACING: *heavy snow in Co. Tipperary*

INDEX OF FIRST LINES

ACKNOWLEDGEMENTS

Grateful acknowledgement is made to the following for permission to reprint the poems in this book. All possible care has been made to trace ownership of selections and to make full acknowledgement. If any errors or omissions have occurred, they will be corrected in subsequent editions.

EAVAN BOLAND 'The Singers', Copyright 1994 © by Eavan Boland reprinted by permission of Carcanet Press Ltd from *Collected Poems* 1995, and by permission of W.W. Norton & Company Inc., from *In a Time of Violence* by Eavan Boland

PAUL DURCAN 'And That Being So', taken from the collection *Westport in the Light of Asia Minor* first published in 1975 by Anna Livia Books, Dublin, in the revised edition 1995 by The Harvill Press. Copyright Paul Durcan 1967, 1975, 1982, 1993, 1995. Reproduced by permission of The Harvill Press

SEAMUS HEANEY 'Thatcher', reprinted by permission of the author and Faber and Faber Ltd, London, and Farrar, Straus and Giroux, Inc., New York, from *Door into the Dark*, 1969 © Seamus Heaney

JOHN HEWITT 'Frost', reprinted by permission of The Blackstaff Press, Belfast

DOUGLAS HYDE: a translation of 'The Mystery', by permission of Mr D. Sealy

PATRICK KAVANAGH 'Plough Horses', reprinted by kind permission of the

Trustees of the Estate of Patrick Kavanagh, c/o Peter Fallon, Literary Agent, Loughcrew, Oldcastle, Co. Meath

LOUIS MACNEICE 'Sligo and Mayo', reprinted by permission of David Higham Associates, London, from 'Natures Notes', *Collected Poems*

DEREK MAHON 'Kinsale', reprinted by permission of the author and The Gallery Press from *Selected Poems* 1991

JOHN MONTAGUE 'Windharp', by kind permission of the author and The Gallery Press, from *Collected Poems* 1995

FRANCIS STUART 'Ireland', reprinted by permission of New Island Books, Dublin

KATHARINE TYNAN 'Winter Morning', reprinted by permission of the literary executors of Pamela Hinkson

W.B. YEATS 'He Wishes for the Cloths of Heaven' and 'The Lake Isle of Innisfree', reprinted by permission of A.P. Watts Ltd on behalf of Michael Yeats